JASON'S JOURNEY

by

VIOLETTE NEWTON

HARP & QUILL PRESS
PALESTINE, TEXAS

Other Books by Violette Newton

Moses in Texas, 1967
The Proxy, 1973
Just My Size, 1975
A Cathedral Ringing, 1976
The Scandal, 1981
Where the Summers Are, 1985
This Is a House to Stand, 1986
All the Druids Are Gone, 1988
Even Hosannas, 1989
Letters from Two Women,
    with Evelyn Corry Appelbee, 1990
All Time Is Now, 1991
The Shamrock Cross, 1993
Because We Dream,
    with Claire Ottenstein, 1994
Art Songs,
    with Gwen Mercer, 1995

Book composition by Lisa Sudela
Art by Meredith Wells
Book design by Brett Barham

Published in the United States of America
    By Harp & Quill Press
        703 S. Magnolia
        Palestine, TX 75801

ISBN 0-9626347-3-5

Visiting The Preserve

An Information Station is located 2.5 miles east of Highway 69-287, and seven miles north of Kountze, Texas, on FM 420, in the Turkey Creek Unit. For information call (409) 246-2337. The Station is open daily from 9 a.m. to 5 p.m. Information can also be obtained by writing to the temporary Headquarters: Superintendent, Big Thicket National Preserve, 3785 Milam, Beaumont, Texas 77701.

Rain, heat, and humidity are integral parts of Big Thicket National Preserve. The average rainfall of 55 inches is well distributed throughout the year. Although the climate is almost tropical, seasonal changes are distinct. Summers are hot and humid with daytime temperatures in the 90's. Winter daytime temperatures, moderated by warm air from the Gulf of Mexico, average in the mid-50's. Many damp, overcast days can be expected, but hard freezes are infrequent. The most pleasant weather for outdoor activities generally occurs in the spring and autumn.

Activities

There are nine hiking and nature trails in five of the twelve Preserve units. Trails range from one quarter mile to eighteen miles in length. The trails provide an overview of the diversity of Big Thicket National Preserve. Guide booklets explain the Kirby Nature Trail and the Sundew Trail. No permits are required for day hikes, but hikers should register and obtain trail maps at the trailheads. The more adventurous may hike cross-country with map and compass.

Visitors can enjoy canoeing, swimming, and fishing. Small watercraft can be launched from various access points along the Neches River, Pine Island Bayou, and Village Creek. Fishing is allowed in all Preserve waters with a valid Texas fishing license. All state fishing regulations apply within the Preserve. The primary species caught in this area are bass, catfish, and white perch (crappie). Hunting and trapping are allowed at designated times and areas with special permits from the Superintendent.

Big Thicket is a diverse outdoor laboratory for nature study. Bird watching is a favorite activity from late March to early May and again in October and November. The keen observer may also see signs of many mammals, reptiles, and amphibians The warm, wet days of spring bring a flush of wildflowers, with many flowers blooming into the summer and fall months. Many visitors enjoy the challenge of discovering and photographing the colorful flowers, fungi, and insects.

Guided hikes, children's programs, lectures, and boat tours are free. Some activities are accessible to the handicapped. For program reservations please call (409) 246-2337.

Accomodations

There are no overnight accommodations within the Preserve. Food and lodging are available in Kountze, Silsbee, Woodville, and Beaumont, Texas. Grocery stores and gas stations dot the roadsides and smaller towns. There are picnic facilities at the Information Station and at trailheads, and some include grills.

Traditional developed campgrounds are not available in the Preserve. However, several public and privately operated campgrounds offer tent and recreational vehicle sites. Minimum impact backcountry camping is allowed in designated camping zones of some Preserve units and on the sandbars in the Neches River. A free Backcountry Use Permit is required. It can be obtained at the Information Station or Headquarters Office prior to your camping trip. Permits are good for five nights.

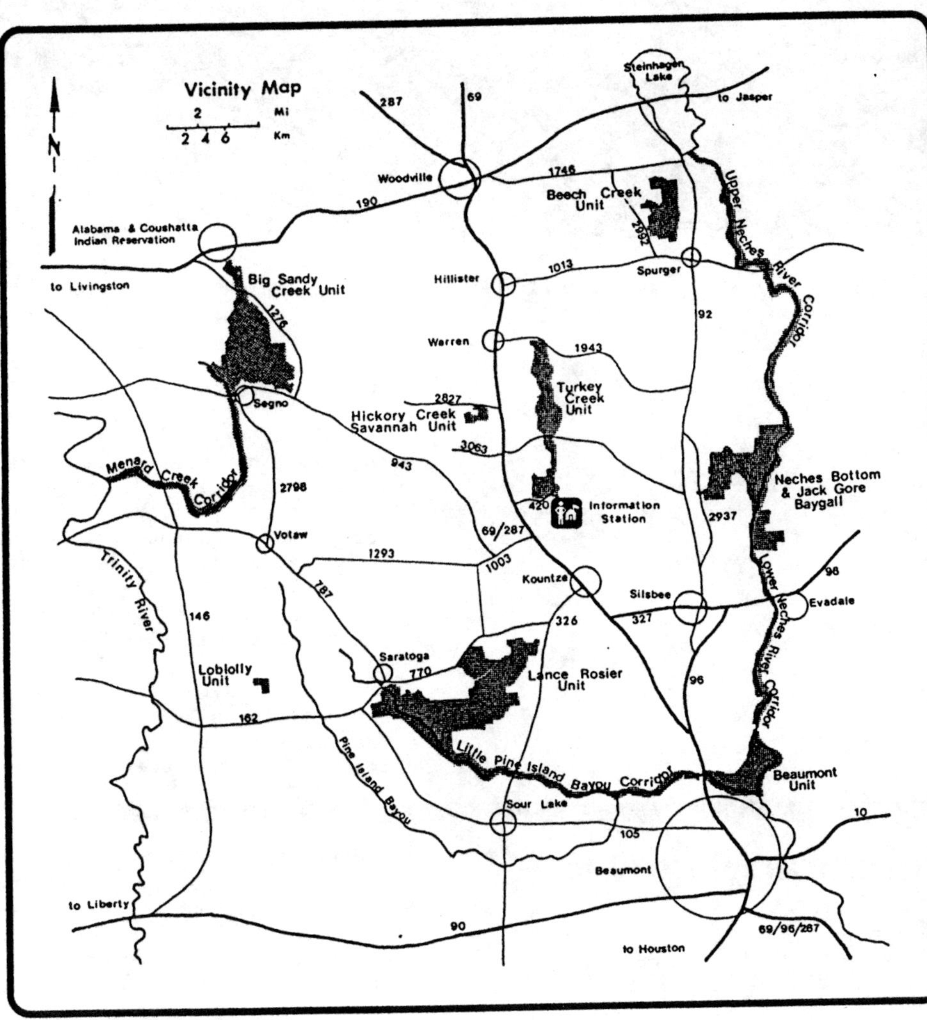

Big Thicket

Biological Crossroads

The Big Thicket is difficult to define. To many, it is a place in Southeast Texas composed of bewildering and mysterious wooded areas. Metaphores such as "an American Ark," "a biological crossroads," and "one of North America's best equipped ecological laboratories" have been used to describe the Big Thicket. The unique quality of the area is not the rarity or abundance of life forms, but the unusual combination of ordinary things. The Big Thicket flourishes with an incredible diversity of plant and animal life.

Big Thicket National Preserve was established in 1974 by Congress to protect remnants of a rich biological resource. The Preserve assures the preservation of representative areas of the original "thicket" once encompassing over three and a half million acres. Big Thicket was designated a <u>Man and the Biosphere Reserve</u> by the United Nations in 1981 attesting to the worldwide significance of Big Thicket resources. As a Biosphere Reserve, Big Thicket is a benchmark of biological diversity that will further humankind's understanding of ecological systems.

Biological influences entwine in the Big Thicket. Eastern forests, central plains, southwest deserts, and southeastern swamps all combine to create a rich tapestry of life. The last Ice Age (10 to 12 thousand years ago) helped to create this diverse phenomenon. Continental glaciers pushed the majority of species south making this region a vast assortment of plant and animal life.

Sloughs of cypress and tupelo are found dramatically close to arid sandhills that support cacti and yucca. Eastern bluebirds may nest near roadrunners. Nearly 1000 plant species are found in the Big Thicket: 85 trees, more than 60 shrubs, 26 ferns and allies, 20 orchids, and 4 of North America's 5 insect-eating plants. This plant diversity exemplifies Big Thicket's importance.

Cultural History

The Big Thicket is as rich in cultural history as it is in natural history. Although early Native Americans hunted in the area, they generally did not venture deep into the thicket. Early settlers tended to avoid the "impenetrable woods," preferring to settle on the edge. The area eventually gained a reputation for lawlessness. The thicket was the lair of murderers, thieves, gamblers, and desperados. During the Civil War some area residents hid out in the woods to avoid military draft.

The tenor of Big Thicket lifestyles persists today in legend and lore, adding richness to the American persona.

Economic exploitation of the Big Thicket began in the 1850's with small scale lumbering. Railroads and sawmills soon followed, determining the fate of the ancient forests. The discovery of oil around 1900 intensified pressures on Big Thicket resources. Drilling for oil continues today in the Preserve. Nearby rice farming flooded previously forested lands while other forests fell before bulldozers. Only small remnants of this once vast region remain intact today.

THE MAKING OF JASON'S JOURNEY

In 1986, Professor Marjorie Morris of Odessa offered a prize for a poem in honor of the Texas sesquicentennial. The work was to be an epic, set in one section of the state, using the people, flora and fauna of the area. JASON'S JOURNEY won that prize.

Chosen as setting was the land around and in the mysterious, folklore-laden Big Thicket of East Texas. It is a place rich in plantlife from widely separated climates, where great trees and undergrowth used to create a hideout for anyone who wished to escape from the known world. Wildlife abounded too in the years after Texas freed itself from old Mexico, which is the approximate time of this work.

An epic poem tells a story, so the poet must have some experience in fiction writing. In this case, the hero had to circulate in the area, and in those days, priests and preachers called "circuit riders" rode around their appointed territories. They knew the people, the plants and animals where they traveled. Not only did they attempt to bring religion to the wilderness, they also brought news of others on the circuit as well as news of the world. The hero of this tale had to be a circuit rider!

Each protagonist has to have an adversary, and the circuit rider's was, of course, evil. In those days, most pioneers believed in a real devil; he has been called Old Evil here. Since all fiction needs conflict, Old Evil will be constantly taunting Jason. But how will he bring him down?

Jason's wife is Sweet Alice, whose character is overdrawn on purpose to show her weakness and delicate nature. She is unfit for hardships of pioneer life. Her early demise is a complication Old Evil needs to plunge Jason into his moral wilderness. As Jason blunders around, he finds himself in the actual wilderness where he stumbles into Old Evil's evil trap.

JASON'S JOURNEY is composed of individual poems written in various poetic forms: free verse, rhymed and metered verse, unrhymed and metered verse, song lyrics, ballad, conversational prose, and old woman's chatterbox vocalizing, a womans' chorus.

I am grateful to Evelyn Corry Appelbee who read every version of the epic
and supported me through thick and thin; to noted folklorist, Dr. Francis
Abernethy, whose suggestions strengthened the plot; to William Barney, a
Poet Laureate of Texas, whose attention to detail helped solve one problem; to
Mary McGaughy, who suggested I eliminate titles originally used on all
poems and title only division pieces; to Dr. A. W. Yates, who told me of his
father's circuit riding days; and to Professor Ruth Scurlock, who told me the
actual story Emily tells of her child's burial.

Also, to my young granddaughter, Arban, who each day came to my home
after school and asked, "What did Jason do today?", to granddaughter, Lisa,
for composition of the book, and to granddaughter, Meredith, for drawings of
Big Thicket flora and fauna. I am deeply indebted to all!

Violette Newton
Beaumont, Texas

TABLE OF CONTENTS

<u>CHARACTERS</u>

Jason, a young circuit rider
Alice, his bride
Neighbors
Nathan, a pioneer
Ebenezer, veteran of San Jacinto
Ruth, his daughter
Caleb, another pioneer
Old Evil, the devil
Emily, a young widow
Old man playing saw
Old woman who offers food
Frenchman
A ghost
Girl at well
Old woman who befriends Jason

MENTIONED IN THE NARRATIVE:

ANIMALS

alligators
ants
Apache doves
beetles
black bear
butterfly
cat
catfish
cow
coyote
crawfish
cricket
deer
dragonfly
fish
fly
fox
frog
hawk
honeybee
horse
hound dog
lizard
moccasin
  (snake)
mockingbird
mosquito
mouse
owl
panther
rabbit
redbird
squirrel
wasp
wolf
woodpecker

TREES

blackgum
cypress
dogwood
hickory
laurel
magnolia
mayhaw
myrtle
pine
pinoak
sweetgum
tupelo
yaupon

PLANTS

berry
bluebonnet
cane
daisy
fern
grape
honeysuckle
hyacinth
jasmine
lily
molds
muscadine
orchid
paintbrush
palmetto
pitcher plant
primrose
rose
smilax
vines
violet

FOODS

beans
buttermilk
clabber
corn
cornpone
cornmeal mush
grapes
greens
gumbo
honey
jambalaya
milk
pork chops
ribs
rhubarb
sassafras
squash
venison

For

Evelyn Corry Applebee

who sings

AMAZING GRACE

with such amazing grace

Stories were told of an epic land
where the streams ran clear
and the trees grew tall,
where the plains flowed wide
as the wide blue sky
and the mountains rose
like thunder! A land
washed clean
by a great, wide Gulf,
and any seeds dropped in this soil
would sprout a miracle! And here
God covered the plainest ground
with flowers of blue and yellow and red,
and the air was songed by the mockingbird.
Men came for land, this wild, free land,
the land Sam Houston freed,
where they would take far more
than they could ever fence.
Men came for greed and came
for freedom too.

But Jason came for God.
In his innocent heart were songs
of the men of old, were truths
long told, and as he drove
the months-long drive
he sang the words
with Alice at his side.
And he believed he believed them.

§§§§§§§§§

Oh, men sang of great Sam Houston
Who came from Tennessee
To lead the Texans in a fight
That soon would set them free.

And Jason came from that state too,
To Texas with his bride.
His aim: to preach the Gospel here
For those who were denied

The word of God because they lived
Too far from any place
Where steeples rose and bells were rung
And sinners prayed for grace.

His Alice was a fragile thing,
A girl with golden hair,
A beauty who had lived a life
That had been free from care.

She learned in Texas she must cook
And make a garden too
And wash and scrub and do the tasks
That girls were meant to do

While Jason rode out night and day
Through weather bad or good
To bring the Word to those who starved,
Who hungered for such food

And when he came back home each time,
He'd tell what he had done:
The marriages, the burials,
The several souls he'd won.

Then as they sat at evening meal
When light began to wane,
Sweet Alice breathed a grateful prayer
That he was home again.

§§§§§§§§§

ALICE'S SONG

"He came to me in April
And love was in his eyes.
He brought me April flowers
Whose color shamed the skies.

"I'd never seen bluebonnets
Until that springtime day
He gathered those blue flowers
Full many miles away.

"And all about the cabin
In Indian pottery,
He placed the bonny blossoms
Oh, everywhere for me!

"But he is off again now,
My Jason's really gone.
And here among the flowers
I wait and wait, alone,
I wait and wait, alone."

§§§§§§§§§

JASON'S PREACHING

And in the morningtime they came
to Nathan's house, and in the afternoon
they came to Nathan's house,
and in the evening,
more came to hear Jason preach.
And they gathered on the dog-trot.
they gathered in the open yard,
and by the light of lighted pine knots,
Jason stood and preached.

And he pressed upon the Lord,
he flailed his arms and called upon
the Lord, he shouted to the Lord
to come down and save the sinners,
to sear away the wretched garments
of their sin and raise them naked
there before the Lord, to lift them
saved and satisfied
in his loving care.

And as he shouted and he sang,
raising sweaty arms unto the Lord,
the sinners came, dropping at his feet,
and they moaned unto the Lord,
begged forgiveness of their lusts,
begged that scales be lifted
from their eyes that they might see
the light and be lifted up.

And Jason pushed back the evil one,
held him off until he moved
into the shadows,
his tail between his legs.

And the people sang and prayed
and shouted with their arms upraised
to heaven, sang their joy unto the Lord
that one of his disciples
had come into the wilderness
to lead them from damnation.

And Jason stood there drenched in sweat,
Jason stood there, wringing wet,
he stood there tall above them
with his arms upraised to heaven
and his face upturned to heaven
while the chastened Evil lingered
deep among the shadows
deep among the pine trees
and plotted his revenge.

§§§§§§§§§

JASON'S SONG

"My love is like a singing lark
And light as air, she sings.
Oh, never such a song was heard
By noblemen or kings.

"When riding through the forest now,
I'll never lonely be
If I know that I soon will fly
To where she waits for me.

"My love is like a singing lark
Who nests within my heart.
Oh, never voice like hers was heard
And we shall never part."

§§§§§§§§§

5

ALICE:

"My mother used to say, 'Those lovely hands!
Use gloves and cremes to keep them soft.'
I pause before the washtub, push back strands
Of blowing hair, then watch a bird aloft

"Cut patterns down the clear, soft Texas sky.
It dips and turns. I think it must look down
On me, land-locked in this far place, then high
Beyond my view, it disappears. My brown

"And water-wrinkled hands dip in the tub
To draw a homespun shirt upon the board.
I pull it back and forth as if to rub
My thoughts into the work, but ever toward

"The wide, free sky my longing eyes return.
I had been once a winging creature too,
Had chosen to come West, had even spurned
A planter's fine proposal for this new

"Adventure. Rinsing, wringing clothes,
  I've pinned
Each piece with love on lines, but oh, I see
The grasses blowing west by rising wind
That my heart tells me comes from Tennessee."

§§§§§§§§§

The days wore into endless weeks
When Alice was alone.
She had much heavy work to do
Because her man was gone.

And so she faded, week by week,
And often was in bed.
The neighbor ladies came to lay
Cool cloths upon her head

And padded soft about the house
And said an humble prayer
That this sweet Alice could survive.
They stroked her golden hair

And waited with her, one by one,
Until her husband came.
Then Alice rose up happily
And blessed his very name.

The neighbor ladies smiled and saw
Their dear and lingering kiss
And whispered to each other that
They'd never seen such bliss.

§§§§§§§§§

Duty called, and reluctantly,
Jason left again to buckle on
his sword and shield against
the evil one, to wage his battles
for the Lord. And one evening far
from home, he stopped at Ebenezer's house,
supped with Ebenezer and his daughter, Ruth,
on cornmeal mush and milk, sat with them
about the board while the candle flickered,
casting shadows, and Ebenezer ruminated
on the San Jacinto victory, how he helped
to take the Mexicans for Sam Houston.

When the old man went outside
to fetch a twig and slice one end
to make a toothbrush, shyly Ruth

7

drew from her pocket a letter
that had been folded and refolded,
spread it on the table, and asked
Jason, please, to read it to her.

Oh, often he was asked to read and write
his people's letters, and this time,
as he saw the opened paper, he knew
it was a letter he had written
weeks ago for Caleb,
when he'd been preaching
down at Caleb's place, a rosy letter,
filled with dignified devotion. So,
not looking up at Ruth, he read the missive
quietly, and her hands flew to her mouth
in some amazement. At the end,
he raised his eyes and looked at her.

"Again," she begged. "Please read it all
again. Then I'll bring ink and quill
that you may pen my answer, that
you may tell good Caleb I am willing."

Jason smiled. The message she thought
Caleb sent was really Jason's own
dear love for Alice, neatly
scripted on the page.

§§§§§§§§§

In the hush of time
in the pineywoods at daybreak
Alice heard birdsong and squirrel chatter,
for God's creatures were about
before the sun appeared.

8

In her long gown, she arose
and moved to the one window
to lean there and look out
on God's Texas.

She hadn't known it would be
like this, and she thought of Tennessee
and home, of her mother weeping
at the gate, her father, grim,
as she rode away with Jason
for the new adventure. She saw
the big house and the long halls,
pictures on the walls, the china,
the spinet, her own bed. It was all
in her mind for her to wander through,
run through. Why was she sad?

She looked up to the high sky
where she thought God was.
She could not see his face,
but her hands came together
in a pleading prayer.

§§§§§§§§§

THE EVIL ONE DANCES

In the pineywoods close by
the evil one chortled, rubbed his hands
in glee and began to dance an ugly jig,
a jump of joy among the pine trees
a jumping up and down of flame
a zig-zag flash of flame
a flash of red
among the underbrush
so everywhere he danced, a fire followed,
everywhere, a hiss of evil joy arose

but Jason, riding home to Alice,
came upon the scene, came in a sudden
whirlwind of his coat, came
in a sudden torrent of his coat,
whipping out the flames
whipping right and left
until he sent Old Evil running
sent him whipped and angry
sent him vowing a revenge
sent him growling a revenge
sent him snorting a revenge
sent him promising revenge.

And riding through the woodlands
he had saved, Jason thought
with joy and satisfaction
of all the souls he'd led
but when he thought of Alice,
his face grew long and sad.
She found no joy in Texas life,
she needed to go home
to Tennessee.

§§§§§§§§§

Jason swept the cabin floor and washed
the clothes and pinned them to the line.
Jason gathered greens for the kettle,
cooked them over fire upon the hearth.
He brought milk up from the neighbor's cow
and hung the bucket in the well to cool.
He propped small pillows about Alice
and read the Scriptures to her.

But Alice thought of other things.
She looked at her rough hands
and remembered that her spinet
sat closed and silent
back in Tennessee.
She thought of china cups and parties
she had missed, she thought of her soft
single bed in her own room at home.

And softly Alice cried
so Jason knelt beside her bed
his arms about her,
and her head came down
upon his shoulder.
"Take me home," she begged,
"take me home."

His countenance was grave.
"When you are strong," he said,
"we'll go." So Alice brightened
and her spirits raised. She dressed
and greeted neighbors who came inquiring
of her health. She laughed and sang
about the house and then insisted
that her husband go again out on the circuit.

§§§§§§§§§

As afternoon was waning, Jason wove
his way into a thicket dense enough
that he must use axe and knife
to hack a passage through. Deep
in lush leaf mold, his feet were sinking,
boots sliding on rocks and roots, so it was
a while before he came into a clearing.
He saw an arrowhead, wondered how far
away the Indians were. Air was pungent
with pine resin and the perfume of hyacinths
that grew along the water's edge. He looked
for wild, sweet grapes, but there were none.

At last, he led his horse to open ground,
and there before him like a picture,
he saw a cabin in the distance. Its door
was open. An ordered garden flourished
by a fence, and he saw a clothesline
where a woman's dress was swinging
in the breeze. As he approached,
a girl with dark brown hair
came to the door and stood.

"Put down that rifle, please," he said.
"I mean no harm. I've ridden many miles
and I need food. Anything will do,
then I'll be on my way. My name
is Jason, ma'am."

Her steady gaze met his. "That's no
concern of mine," she told him,
but Jason asked again that she lay down
the gun. She stood her ground. "I'll
hold it on you if I please." He saw
her eyes were dark, and dark
with fear.

He shrugged. "If you shoot me,
my only armor is the Lord."

"My God!" she blazed. "There is no God!"

"By God, there is a God! Put down
that rifle, girl, and talk to me.
What causes all this anger?"

"I'll not talk with strangers, man!
Go on! And I've no use for piety.
It never got me anywhere. I'll
have no dealings with your God.
He took Cyrus."

"Cyrus?"

"My man. He died of fever. If he had
been with old Sam Houston, I might forgive
his death and have some pride in it. But
fever! It was a senseless death God sent.
You've never loved someone enough
to understand what I am saying?"

Jason's voice was soft. "Oh, yes.
I think I understand. I have a wife.
I know I am the luckiest man alive
to have her. She gave up everything
to come out here with me. And life
is hard for her, very hard for her here."

The rifle lowered, but the girl's face
was stern. "And how," she asked,
"would you be feeling about God
if he took her away?" Jason's mouth
dropped open. "You think it couldn't
happen? So I thought too. Then God
took small Amanda."

"Amanda?"

"She got the fever from her father.
But I'll not talk of Mandy now. Oh,
come on in, I'll get your supper...
there's enough. My name is Emily."

She moved into the room, and Jason
followed. He looked up to the mantel.
"Books!" he cried. "What have we here?"
She smiled shyly then, as he went
to the shelf. "The Bible, Shakespeare,
Bobby Burns." He turned to her.
"You've read any of them?"

She nodded as she set bowls
on the crude, rough table. "They're all
I have of Papa's. He brought them
when he came from Alabam. I've read them,
every word. What else to do when nights
are long and there's a candle
or a hearth fire making light?"

He came up to the table where she ladled
stew into the bowls. "You're as brave
a young woman as I've seen out here,
brave to be living all alone."

"Not brave. Sometimes I'm scared,
but this is my land, my home.
Where else to go?"

"Miss Emily, when I come around again,
I'll stop to ask you how you are,
if that's all right."

She lowered then her eyes and nodded,
"Yes."

A week out on the circuit, Jason
stopped at Nathan's house to preach
when one lone rider rushed
into the yard to call Jason home.

§§§§§§§§§

As Alice lay dying
The lone owl was crying
And Jason went for the doctor that night.
In the dews and the damps
And the miserable swamps
The moon never seemed so silvery bright.

But the slither of snake
In the lonesome canebrake
And the eerie cries of panthers nearby
Caused his blood to turn chill
And his blue eyes to fill
At the notion that Alice could die.

He crossed river and creek
In his journey to seek
Help for Alice, and high in the trees,
Desperate prayer after prayer
He sent up on the air
But they wafted away on the breeze.

The old doctor was out,
He was nowhere about,
So down through the dark and the gloom,
Jason rode home alone
With his hope nearly gone
For he had a feeling of doom.

Honeysuckle spread on
Its sweet incense at dawn,
But the sun hid its face in a cloud.
His heart jolted: "Why?"
But he could not deny
Neighbor ladies were sewing a shroud.

Now, Jason thrashed and he cried
That his young wife had died...
He forgot every lesson he'd taught,
And he found no relief
From his sorrow and grief
That sweet Alice's passing had brought.

§§§§§§§§§

The hammers are rapping,
Now rapping and tapping
   to build for sweet Alice
   her final home.
The shovels are digging,
Oh, digging and digging
   to dig her a grave
   in the sandy red loam.

While Alice lies sleeping,
While Jason bows, weeping,
   the neighbors come close
   and hover around.
But the only sound here
From far and from near
   is that echoing,
   echoing sound.

The hammers are rapping,
Now rapping and tapping
   to build for sweet Alice
   her final home.
The shovels are digging,
Oh, digging and digging
   to make her a grave
   in the sandy red loam.

§§§§§§§§§

17

WOMEN:

"Who will he have
To comfort him now,
Who will he have
To warm him in bed?
Death-dews have settled
On Alice's brow
For, Alice, sweet Alice
Is dead dead dead.

"Who'll cook cornpone
And beans for him now,
Who will he have
To warm him in bed?
Sandy-haired Jason,
Your nights will be cold,
Blue-eyed Jason, there're
Sad times ahead.

"Who will he have
To comfort him now,
Who will he have
To warm him in bed?
Death-dews have settled
On Alice's brow
For Alice, sweet Alice
Is dead dead dead."

§§§§§§§§§

Easing the ropes down,
men lower the pine box
into the red earth

and the sky-blue sky
inverts its bowl of heat
deep in the hollow
while the sun beats its drum
on the pines.

"Who will give the eulogy?" one asks.
    Jason shakes his head.

"Who will chant the final psalm?"
    But Jason turns away.

"Who will sing *Shall We Gather
    at the River?"*
    But Jason says, "God took Alice.
    I'll speak to him no more."

Then the brethren ease the ropes down
and the brethren let down sweet Alice
inch by awful inch by awful inch
into the six feet of red earth,
and the brethren sing out the psalm
of the house of many rooms
and they sing *Amazing Grace*
there in the terrible heat, there
in the bitter sunlight, there in
the sun of the pineywoods, there by
the grave of sweet Alice.

And they toss in the earth to earth
and the dust to dust
and the women come, dropping
bluebonnets and Indian "paint brush"
and primroses onto the pine box
deep
in the red earth

and one and then another
of the shovels

lifts in sunlight,
tossing red earth,
tossing red earth,
tossing, tossing
red earth
onto the pine box
deep
in the red earth

and the people lead Jason away
while a woman comes with a rose bush
and plants it at the grave
of sweet Alice.

§§§§§§§§§

WOMEN:

"Preacher Man, Preacher,
Let go of your grief!
You can't throw away
Your faith and belief.

"You who have shouted
And sung the Lord's praise
Must know he never
No, never will raise

"Alice, sweet Alice
Like Lazarus. Oh,
Preacher Man, Preacher,
Not get up and go

"Down in the Valley...
He'll walk there with you
And lead you to light.
You told us it's true."

Evil is watching
Oh, not far away,
Denying each word
The good people say.

§§§§§§§§§

JASON'S CURSE

"Through the long sleety nights
And the mud and the rain
I have gone out to comfort
My people in pain

"But I made empty promises,
Told them bold lies,
Though I believed all I told them
Was wonderfully wise.

"And down through the weeks
And the months...as I went
Performing God's mission
On which I was sent

"He was coaxing sweet Alice
To leave me, I know.
He was tempting sweet Alice
To leave me and go!

"Oh, God, I shall curse you!
No longer I'll pray,
For you took my sweet Alice,
You took her away."

> *Now, close behind Jason*
> *There comes a low hiss.*
> *Old Evil laughs*
> *And dances in bliss.*

§§§§§§§§§

Lord of the skies
and Lord of the hill
Jason is drinking
He's lost his will

He's lost his will
He's lost his way
Jason is drinking
Weeping away

Weeping away
Lost his belief
Jason is drinking
Drowning in grief

Drowning in grief
Touch him again
Jason is drinking
Drinking his pain.

> *Holding his sides*
> *Laughing in glee*
> *Old Evil calls this*
> *His victory.*

§§§§§§§§§

Fog in the hollow,
the morning lies shrouded
deep in a mist
that blinds Jason's eyes.

Where is his Alice?
He hears her voice calling,
he wanders and searches,
she's lost in the fog.

Deep in the hollow
the branches are snapping.
The wild berry vine
Catches his legs.

He falls on a stump
flowered with molds,
cuts his chin on it,
lies weeping in fern.

Alice, oh Alice,
where have you gone?
Jason, poor Jason
lies here alone.

§§§§§§§§§

Deep in the damps
Jason wakes to the moon
To the stream flowing by
Mumbling its rune

Hears through his torment
A lonesome hound's bark
Rise to the moon
Riding high in the dark.

Staggering up,
He sees Alice there
Dressed all in white
With a rose in her hair

Runs through the fiddleheads
Calling to her.
The fox in his den
Starts up with a stir.

The rabbit, the dove
Quiver in bed.
The whole forest knows
Sweet Alice is dead.

Jason runs to the white
Apparition there,
The girl that he loved
With a rose in her hair

Falls in the dogwood
Whitely abloom
And sobs in his deep
And griefstricken gloom.

§§§§§§§§§

Morning has come and Jason awakens
At the foot of the dogwood tree.
Staggering up and reaching for branches,
He wonders where he can be.

Stumbling onward, he falls on his face
In the green and limpid frog pond.
Suddenly sobered, he stares at his house
All open and lonely beyond.

Why should he stay there when Alice is gone,
Oh, why not be off on his way!
He bends to his sleeve, wipes down his face
And gets up to a different day.

Now turning, he moves away from his house
Away from his Bible book too,
Away from the hearth where Alice had sat,
Away from the life that he knew

25

Away from the box buried deep deep deep
And the scarred red earth where she lies.
Wiping a tear, he starts walking away
And he shakes his fist at the skies.

But off from the pathway,
down in the woods,
Old Evil looks on and he smiles.
He'll think of a way to entrap this one
Before he's gone many more miles.

§§§§§§§§§

Wandering, Jason staggers, red-eyed
in the woods, but he stumbles
onto Emily's land and comes
upon her in the garden.

"Stay back!" she cries. "Who are you?"

"I'm lost. Can't you see?"

"Oh, I remember you. You're lost
in more ways than one. What happened?"

"I'm lost."

She leans her hoe against the wall
takes his arm and leads him
into the house, gives him food
and makes a pallet near the hearth
where he falls asleep. At morning time
when he awakens, he looks, startled,
to the room and its rough furnishings.

"How came I here?" he asks.
Then he sees Emily.

"You just appeared. I took you in."

He sits up, holds his throbbing head.
"Alice is gone, Alice is dead. I've
been drinking...I never drink."

"Alice? Your wife?"

He begins to cry. "She was mine, and
I brought her here where God took her
away. I would I hadn't loved her so;
she'd still be living back
in Tennessee."

"You need some food, man. Stop crying.
It does no good. Get up, and get
yourself together."

"Can't you understand?"

"I ought to. God took my man
and took my child too. She got
the fever after Cyrus died of it.
My little one, my only one.
I buried her myself. It was
a shallow grave, all I could dig,
and in the night, the starving wolves
were coming."

Jason is shaking, hands trembling
as she tells her tale.

"All night long at the window, I
Leveled my gun on Mandy's grave.
The wolves were near, I heard them cry,
And I was never brave.

"I moaned my fears as they came close

And hungering, they closer came.
They waited, still, and my blood froze
As shaking, I took aim.

"They came again, but cautiously.
I cried, I gave a piercing scream.
The beasts fell back, their game with me
A gruesome nightmare dream.

"I fired again and they yelped back
A little way, not full retreat.
My hearth fire glowed, I knew the pack
Would run from rushing heat.

"I set a bench in fire to burn.
I grabbed it, ran outside and gave
The thing a heave and saw it turn
And fall on Mandy's grave.

"I took a footstool and a chair
And set them burning on the grate,
And running, carried them out there,
And oh, the hour was late!

"I ran with quilted coverlets
And threw them on the rising fire.
They broke apart in little bits,
The flame was like a gyre!

"The wolves went loping fast away,
They howled the dark with their alarms.
I dragged inside, and weeping, lay,
The empty cradle in my arms."

Wiping tears, she sinks down on the bench.
He rises, goes to her, to touch her on
the shoulder. She looks up. "I did

what I must do, that's all. And then,
I had an empty house, an empty life.
I made the benches and the table,
gathered what I could to keep me warm."

He stares dully at her, stares away.
"God robbed you as he robbed me.
I'm sorry sorry, Emily."

§§§§§§§§§

THE BIG THICKET

Time was intrigued here
in the mystery years
when the world was young,
and wandering lonely among the woods,
Time came to a clearing and looked down,
deep down in a narrow stream
and saw the clear blue skies look back
through the softly rippling waves.

And Time looked up to the cool tree shade
and saw leaf patterns against leaf patterns
of oak and sweet gum and cypress there
and dogwood and tupelo anchored deep
in the veins, the very veins of earth
where lilies and daisies and violets
sprang. And all about in the pungent air
were butterflies' wings, applauding.
And low were the sounds of birds
and squirrels, and the movements
of deer in woods.

So Time decided to stay,
to bid goodbye to the rushing world
where clocks tick fast
and people themselves wind up
like the ticking clocks.

The trees grew tall and the Thicket dense.
To close in a world where Time
still wanders free
and sits and meditates.

§§§§§§§§

Deep in Big Thicket
Jason is walking
down where the cypresses
stand in the baygall

down where the laurel
magnolia and mayhaw
quarrel for footing

and where the sweet gum
pin oak and black gum
march by the bayous

where the alligator
opens his jaws
and the black snake
and moccasin swim

and the muscadine climbs
over all, weaving and binding
into a wicket the steady growth
of Big Thicket.

No longer the black coat,
black hat of the preacher,
no longer the Word
to sing from his lip,
for instead of the Good Book,
he wears a pistol,
a pearl-handled pistol
there on his hip.

§§§§§§§§§

31

The evil one knows this
Old wilderness, so
He leads Jason down
Where no man should go.

Confused in the thicket,
Jason loses the trail
Cuts through some ty vines,
Myrtle and yaupon

Comes to a cabin
Shambled and old
Where a bearded old man
Sits playing a saw.

But crack! in the underbrush,
Jason's foot tries to pass
And snap! go the twigs
As he moves through their mass.

The man grabs a rifle,
Aims it out there
And Jason comes out,
His hands in the air.

An old woman comes
From housewifery tasks,
Looks out at Jason
And she kindly asks

"Who are you stranger,
And what do you seek?
Danger lies nearby
In bayou and creek.

"Snakes are all hidden
And wait for you there.
Lost in Big thicket,
You'll meet the black bear.

"Turn around, stranger,
And head out of here.
Rifle's aimed at you
So don't you come near. "

Behind him, a laugh
Behind him, a leer
Behind him, a smirk.
Old Evil is near.

The woman is kind
The woman is good.
The woman is kind,
She offers him food.

§§§§§§§§§

"I can offer you cornpone
    and clabber and greens
I can offer you cornpone
    and clabber and greens
I can offer you cornpone
    and clabber and greens
For Mister, that's all we got.

"Sometimes we have fatback
    and porkchops and ribs
Sometimes we have fatback
    and porkchops and ribs
Sometimes we have fatback
    and porkchops and ribs
Mister, that's when he kills a hog.

"If you don't like clabber
    you can have buttermilk
If you don't like clabber

you can have buttermilk
If you don't like clabber
    you can have buttermilk
Mister, we ain't got coffee or tea.

"If you don't like buttermilk,
    Mister, I say
If you don't like buttermilk,
    Mister, I say
If you don't like buttermilk,
    Mister, I say
You can have a sup of branch water.

"But you'd best eat fast
And be on your way."

§§§§§§§§§

JASON'S LAMENT

"I shake my fist at the sky
and I have no remorse.
I shall find my own way,
I shall set my own course.

"No longer God, my compass,
No longer, God, my source,
I shall find my own way,
I shall set my own course."

 But whose voice is this voice
 That comes from Jason's throat?
 Has Evil entered him
 To sing a dismal note?

    §§§§§§§§§

"Here on a pallet I lie
On this cabin gallery,
And through the black-dark trees,
 the sky
Looks down accusingly.

"I stare, and I find a star
That fixes its eye on me.
How can a light that shines so far
Look down accusingly?

"Here on a pallet am I
Through a stranger's charity.
My blood itself beats in my heart
Accusingly. "

    §§§§§§§§§

Jason sits down
To rest on the rocks,
He takes off his boots
And he takes off his socks.

He savors the feel
Of the forest air
When suddenly out
Of its hidden lair

A stump-tailed cotton-
Mouth mocassin slides.
Writhing and twisting,
It comes as it glides

But a shot rings out!
Jason jumps up to see
The old snake collapse
By a cypress knee

And a man comes out
Of the deep dark wood
And says, "I kilt him
and I knowed I could

"So come along, man,
You come home with me
And sit and tell us
Just who you be."

§§§§§§§§§

FRENCHMAN:

"Cabin in de wood,
Cabin in de pine
All drape aroun wif
De muscadine vine.

"Oui, we got two house.
Each one be little,
Join wif de dog-trot
Dare in de middle.

"Wife cook outside
If wedder be good.
Mah fran, you goin like
Dat ole Cajun food!

"Crawfish an catfish
Caught in de bayou
An chicken gumbo
An jamabalaya!

"Dare mah ole wife-mate
In red bandanna.
Oui, man, we do come
Fum Louisiana.

"A long time ago
An far fum dis worl,
A man make a pass
At mah own sweet girl.

"Hot in de head, me!
I didn like dat,
So I hit him good
But he knock me flat

"An I shot him dead,
So we had to come here.

Mah fran, we got peace
For many long year.

"It's a place to hide,
It's a place to stay.
Nobody ain't goin
Send us away."

While the Frenchman talks,
Glad of company,
Jason's heart dissolves
In its misery.

§§§§§§§§§

Jason pauses in the woods
for he hears a small sound, sees
a shadow flying through trees.
Is it the ghost of a bird he heard?
He sees it, or he thinks he sees it.

Is it legend, this ivory-billed
woodpecker? But he saw it.
He blinks and it flies away
into the dark tangle
of his mind.

§§§§§§§§§

The thicket is dark
The thicket is green,
A man enters here
And never is seen.

If he wants to hide
If he wants to wait,

38

The thicket will close
Though it has no gate.

Jason walks around
As afternoon comes.
He moves toward a tree
And the old tree hums

Oh, the old tree hums
And it seems alive
So he backs off fast
From that honey hive

Oh, he backs off fast
And he seems to lope
Down a little path
On a gentle slope

With the bees behind
Till he steps into
The gloom and the mud
Of a widening slough

And there in the dark
Of his hopelessness
Jason seems to sink
In his own distress

> *While lurking nearby*
> *A tupelo tree*
> *Old Evil's laughing,*
> *But silently.*

§§§§§§§§§

Jason wanders off
To an open place,

And down in the creek
He sees his face,

Down through the waters
Clear and still
Where the sleek fish come
And the green frog will

Submerge himself
In a world as old
As the world itself,
So still and cold.

Jason looks down
And his own grave face
Is a picture framed
In the ferns' green lace

Is a picture caught
In a place where he
Has glimpsed God's green
Eternity.

He stands transfixed
In a moment there,
And he almost says
An old old prayer.

§§§§§§§§§

Startled, Jason stumbles on a skull
entwined in smilax
so its white gleams dully
through the weave of vines.

He pauses there to wonder
what those eyes saw
through these vacant windows,
what words issued past
the broken, grinning teeth,
what thoughts roved that cranium.

Why had this man come here?
How long has he lain
where people walk
and turn their faces
as they pass? Where are
the other bones?

His own head reels with pictures
from his past. He could so easily
lie down in thicket or in creek
and end the pictures rushing
through his mind.
He thinks how this could be

but a wasp with spotted wings
passes by. He watches as it goes,
small and busy and alive.
He sighs and walks on past
the skull as others do.

§§§§§§§§§

Moonlight streams down between trees
and bathes in soft rays the sensuous orchids
and lilies blooming in the night. Jason
is on the "Ghost Road" where an eerie
light bounces from place to place,
a phosphorescent glare. His teeth chatter,
his hands are shaking as if he has an ague.
Furtively, stealthily he moves. He stumbles,
falls and gets up. His arms are snagged
by thorns. And out of air, a ghost appears.
Jason trembles as the apparition begins
to tell his story.

"My Lucy lies in the thicket now,
Her Ezra lies beside.
He was her wedded husband too
And she, his lonely bride.

"He made her chairs of hickory wood,
He bought a ring of gold,
But Lucy yearned for young sweet love
And Ezra's heart was cold.

"Sweet Lucy gazed from East to West
As they went out one day.
Her husband's eyes looked straight ahead
But Lucy looked my way!

"And in the evening more than once
While crusty Ezra slept,
Oh, to my arms she quickly came
And in my arms she wept.

"I held her tenderly and close,
I stroked her coal-black hair.
I gave her all my heart's true love
Till Ezra found us there.

"He shot her through her snow-white breast,
I grabbed his smoking gun
And riddled him with bleeding holes
And when that deed was done

"Her brothers came and buried them
Together, side by side.
Their blameless kinsman, Ezra, and
His faithless black-haired bride!

"They called me robber, called me thief,
They drenched my name with gall
And hung me from this old oak tree
Until my bones did fall

"So other lads gave me a kick,
They laughed in fiendish glee!
But oh, their black hearts wanted her
And oh, they envied me!"

The apparition suddenly vanishes
before Jason's eyes. Far far
in the lonesome woods, he hears
a long and frightening cry. Is it
an owl, or is it Evil, rapturous
over this lost soul?

§§§§§§§§§

JASON:
"Old black oak, birds are nesting
in your arms as I would rest
in God's again.

"What is my life worth now?
I have lost everything I had.
I have never felt so low

43

I have never felt so bad.

"There is nothing left for me,
There is nothing I can do
But wander aimlessly
The lonesome long days through."

But tripping through the shadows,
Evil thinks that he can win:
"I'll tempt you, oh, I'll tempt you
With a lovely sin!"

§§§§§§§§§

Wild orchids hang
from the feathery trees
and pitcher plants spring
from the ground. Flowering molds
of brown and gold cluster against
an old stump mound. But down
in the baygall at morning time,
it is dim as the twilight hour.
The tupelo trees and the cypresses
close out the light
in this darksome bower
and the evil one wanders there.

He must think of a way to use his power
to conquer the wandering preacher-man.
He thinks and he thinks
and his looks are sour. Deep
in the baygall, dim and dank,
the evil one plots his ploy.
He thinks and he thinks
his cunning thoughts,
and he thinks a woman there.
He thinks her lips and he thinks

her eyes, he thinks a wild rose
in her hair...he claps his hands
and he sees the thin short gown
she'll surely wear. The gown
slips down and leaves a shoulder bare.

§§§§§§§§§

Jason has walked about, hopelessly lost,
hungry and thirsty, when he looks up
and sees in the distance a mirage,
a water well where a young woman
is drawing up a wooden bucket,
water spilling over its tilted side.
He is in the deep woods; how does
this girl and this well happen
to be here? He rubs his eyes,
not quite believing. The young woman
is beautiful-clear skin, a radiant smile,
curly black hair. She speaks as he asks
for a drink.

"The water from my well
Is sweet as morning dew.
I'm drawing up a bucketful,
And there's enough for you.

"Sure, I'll give you a sup,
There's plenty of it here,
But if you try any mischief,
My pappy will appear.

"The thicket's full of eyes
The rifle's always ready,
And let me tell you, stranger-man,
Aim is awful steady!

45

"You like the way I look?
I laugh, for I like you too!
I like your shaggy sandy hair
And oh, those eyes of blue!

"You like my big black eyes
And you like my curly hair,
You like my smiling warm red lips?
They're made for kissing there!

"But oh, you lovely thing,
I could give you more than this!
My pappy's gone out hunting, dear,
And I am made for bliss!"

§§§§§§§§§

Jason stares at the girl, stares
at the laughing, taunting eyes,
the lips pursed temptingly before him.
He feels weak, he trembles, blood pounds
in his throat and temples. He takes
one step backward, for he must leave,
but the girl steps forward with the cup.
Her face has changed to a face of innocence.
She extends the cup and he is thirsty,
he drinks deeply, wipes his mouth on his hand,
extends the cup, and as their hands meet,
her skin burns against his, his eyes blaze,
his breath rasps through his parted lips.

He turns abruptly, murmuring almost
inaudibly his thanks, but an irresistible
force binds his feet to the ground.
He has touched a woman, he is mesmerized,
and he stands there, blinded to all sense
of will, all but the hand reaching out

46

to lead him into the dark forest,
far far into the dark forest, deep
into the depths of the dark forest
through a ruffle of leaves, over
fallen limbs, into the stillness
like the stillness of night, where,
slowly, she draws him down with her
to the ashy leaves, to the soft coolness
of the forest bed, to her arms about him,
her lips as his own, until his hands move
feverishly at her face, move over her face,
his hands caress her face, stroke her hair,
his hands are at her clothing, his hands,
his hands searching, seeking, finding.
He loses himself in all
but the subliminal core of self,
so he cries out in the dream
of primitive drama Alice never knew,
all animal in this wilderness, a savage,
satisfying kind of revenge on himself,
as violent as passions of the ancients
who loved in tents of goat skins
or under desert stars. He sinks his teeth
into her skin, so she cries out,
damning him to hell.

Struggling, she tries to free herself
from this mad man, but he keeps her
until he falls back, silent, spent,
and he sleeps.

His eyes open. Was he so weak
that he fell here and was dreaming?
He sees shadows, he thinks he sees shadows
in this dark place...who is creeping
toward him? He thinks he hears laughter.
Is it Old Evil in triumph? Jason
lunges at a shadow, wrestling
with air. His head is swimming,

sweat runs down from his forehead.
His hand goes to his unfired gun,
lying there beside him. He fires it,
reels back, the shot astounds the air.
Earth trembles in the shouting silence.
Gun drops from his hand, falls through
tangled vines and deep leaf mold,
down where ants and beetles
weave their tunnels.

Blinking, he stares, frowns.
Was the girl here? Was he alone
in the dark forest? Was the girl here?
Has he lost himself in moments lifted
out of a lifetime of learned patterns?
He looks down, sees the crushed wild rose
lying in the ashy leaves. He knows
the girl was here. He is damned
to everlasting hell. Head in hands,
he looks dumbly into deepening dark.
Air is still, there is no sound
but leaf fall. The forest
holds its secrets.

> *Now Evil calls his cohorts.*
> *He claps his hands and dances,*
> *and the forces of Evil follow,*
> *stepping high, laughing hideous,*
> *stormy laughter. Lightning streaks,*
> *thunder rolls and growls, rain*
> *pours in sheets, old trees*
> *crash and fall.*

Jason crouches in the storm, arms
about his head, his body quivering
with fear. Is hell so near?

§§§§§§§§§

His eyes open warily, wearily
on a wet world, and he sees
a single violet blooming velvet
in the mesh of leaves.
He speaks to it.
"How came you, hiding in the dark?
I never saw you other days. I was
too busy with God's work
to see God's work."

A dragonfly lights on a mottled limb.
Its iridescent wings take light
in rainbow hues. Jason draws
himself up, wipes his dirty face
on his dirty sleeve, and blinking,
faces the indignity of himself.

Sunlight falls in ribbons
through the trees, drops
of last night's rain glisten
on limbs and leaves. He rises
stiffly, brushing litter from
his clothes, and wiping his face
once more, walks slowly from
his forest bed. What can he do?
Where can he go? He keeps brushing
at his clothes as if to brush away
his stain. He quivers. That girl.
Had he dreamed her, or was she real?
She was real. Hands to his face,
he shivers. He is doomed to hell.
Other men have confessed such sins
to him and not been devastated...
if only he had kept the pistol,
or...he could lose himself
in the creek.

He stumbles on, eyes to soggy ground,
until he comes into a clearing

and comes upon an old woman, hoeing
in a row of okra plants. "Lost?"
she asks. "Well, them that come
from the outside usually are. Go sit
a spell in the swing over there,
and rest. I'll lay my hoe aside.
Sun's too hot this time of day.
Okra'll wait.

"You want some sassafras tea? Get you
a gourd and go in the cabin and take
a sup. And come out here and talk
to me. I ain't had no one to talk with
for awhile. I entertain myself making
songs and rhymes. I'll just rest
in the rawhide chair.

"You found it? Well, bring it out
and sip it slow. I see you took
some cornpone too. That's good,
for you look like you ain't et
in a while. What'd you do, sleep
in the woods? Come, sit down.
Look at that squirrel! He knows
you're strange around here. He'll
eat out o' my hands most times.
Other creatures come too. I been here
so long, nothin ain't scared o' me.
No, I can't remember no other place.
I come here as a child, been here
all my life.

"Some fellow come through once,
lookin to learn of trees and plants
and soil. I let him stay
in my little old cabin out back.
He said he thought the waters was over
all this land in olden olden times,
just like it says in the Book:

`The Lord gathered the waters in one
place.' What's that you say?
That he `let the dry land appear"?
why, you know Scriptures too!

"How'd you come to come out here?
You ain't huntin, are you?
You ain't got no gun. Just lookin
to see what you can see? Well,
there's a plenty o' that here.
From where you come, tell me,
what year was it out there?"

Jason looks at her with glazed,
feverish eyes...he doesn't know
what year, what month, what day.

"Young man, there's a washtub out back
in my old cabin. Go draw some water
from the well and make a fire
to heat it. You need a good soakin.
I'll bring you soap and old clean clothes.
You look bad. There's cot and covers
in the cabin. Why don't you clean
yourself and sleep?"

And after some soothing moments
of hot water, Jason falls upon
the cabin cot and sleeps the sleep
of the newly dead.

Day passes into evening and evening
into night when the mockingbird sings,
owl cries, and the field mouse runs
through a chorus of crickets.
Moon rises over the stream, frog
croaks at the edge of the stream,
but Jason sleeps, and sleeps all night.

When sky behind the pines is streaked
with morning's gold, his body jerks
awake, eyes open, and he sits up,
puzzled. Where is he? He looks around,
trying to remember. He is clean,
he is sleeping in a bed. Through
the doorway, he sees the old woman
in her garden. He lies back again
as blackness clouds his vision.
He is weak. Arm over eyes,
he lies there.

Alice is gone, he has blamed God
for her passing, just as Emily
blamed God for her losses. He has
cursed God, he has sinned, he has
sinned with a woman. He groans,
for that memory wipes out everything
he believed before. He is lightheaded,
the walls, the walls, the cabin walls
begin to move, to go around, around.

He thinks he sees Jacob's ladder,
a scene he has used in sermons
many times. It is linking earth
to sky, and he hears his own voice
intone, "And behold! the angels
of the Lord ascending and descending
on it." His vision is dizzy
with the spectacle as the room goes
around and around. He holds his head,
tries to sit up but falls back,
and the room spins around and around.

In bushes behind the cabin,
Evil loiters, grinning.

Angels! Has God sent a sign?
Tightly Jason closes his eyes,
his face contorted.

> *Evil begins a little jig,*
> *hunching his shoulders, hand*
> *over his mouth to suppress*
> *laughter.*

The old woman looks in at the door,
shakes her head. "Young man,
you look bad sick. Here, let me feel
your forehead. Why, you got fever!
I'll go fix some herb tea for you."

> *Evil scowls. Jason is his prize.*
> *Is the old fool trying to save him?*

§§§§§§§§§

How many days has he been there in bed,
writhing in fever? How many nights
has he listened through a gauze
of delusion to the old woman's songs
as she bathed his face with cool water?
He remembers her singing always made him
feel easy before he drifted off
in a field of fever again, floating
on waves of undulating heat and chill.
Parts of her singing sometimes
came back to him:

"I came to sweet Texas
For my piece of land,
I came here for my peace of mind.
I got me a stake, all I could take,
And sweet love I also did find."

But when she repeated the last line,
he would cry out and beg her to stop.

Now dark falls and night noises begin,
not in a harmony of sounds to his ear,
pulsing with fever. Sounds rise
and fall in the mockingbird's melodies,
shout at him in the staccato barking
of dogs, irritate him in the needled
whine of mosquitoes. He listens
until the hum of sounds sends him
into a fog of sleep where he hears
the old woman singing again
and her voice is sweet.

"Oh, would I were young in the springtime,
Oh, would I were willowy slim.
I would wait by the willows in springtime,
I would wait by the willows for him."

His fever takes him away and back
to Tennessee, where his family
is seated beneath the arching ribs
of a high ceiling, listening to talk
of miracle and mystery he does not
understand. He sees light streaming
down in bits of color, forming broken
pictures that grip his childish mind:
the nailprint hands, crown of thorns,
wings and the torn heart. There is
no such place in the wilderness.

The old woman hums again; he turns
restlessly in sleep until he is besieged
with tremors. Turning, turning,
he cries out, for now before him in air,
old Jacob of the Scriptures wrestles with
a stranger. Jason buries his face
in his pillow to close out the scene

but the vision invades his mind.
Tossing, twisting, turning,
he sees it in broken colors
of that gothic window at home,
sees it in shades of mist
even unto the first pale morning
light, and his fever is over.

He lies motionless, his mind clear,
but the figures still move above him
in veiled air. Old Jacob's figure
comes apart in mists, but the stranger
turns, turns about to show his face.
Jason grabs the bedside, lying rigid,
mouth open in astonishment, not quite
believing, then awestruck, for he knows
the face before him...he dares not look,
for he knows he looks into the face
of God, into the pale face of God,
now radiant, now translucent,
now no longer there.

He sits up, heart beating in his throat.
He stares around. If this were dream...
but his mind is clear now. His lungs
drink in great gulps of air.
He hears his name being called.
He looks to the open doorway,
but no one is near...he is alone,
yet someone called him, called his name.
And some new feeling enters him, some
burst of energy, exuberance, purpose.

Impaled upon the spirit,
he feels himself ignite.

He must go.
But what is that eerie cry he hears?
He sits there on the bedside, very still.

He listens to loud howling in nearby woods.
Whoever or whatever makes that cry
must be running fast, away.
Some animal, whipped by another
of its kind? Some creature
who has lost a fight? The sound
diminishes as the creature runs down
into the closing wilderness.

Jason rises to test his legs.
He can stand. His clean clothes
are hanging on a nail on the wall,
and he must try to dress. He smiles.

He must go.

§§§§§§§§

JASON'S FULL CIRCUIT

The world's not changed; he thought
it would be. He sees the rutted roads
he once rode on, he notices
the smallest flower, the songs
in trees, the freshness
of the morning breeze,
and on his lips,
thanksgiving whispers words.

Then, in a little clearing
on a little rise of ground,
he sees the wooden crosses
and the people gathered around
a box they will lower
in the ground.

He pauses there to contemplate
the scene. Has God prepared
this gathering to greet his eyes,
to test his strength? He sees
the people darkly dressed,
all bowing to the raw
hand-shoveled earth.

He draws quite near as impulse
moves his feet. He hesitates
until he hears a voice call out,
    "Who shall say the eulogy?
    Who shall chant the final psalm?
    Who shall sing *Shall we Gather
      at the River?*

When no one answers,
Jason comes nearer and says, "I will,"
and looking deeply in the eyes

of all who stare at him,
he begins his eulogy.

§§§§§§§§§

"These are the hands that in the long ago
brought blue and yellow Texas flowers,
an offering for her.

"These the hands that caught the newborn
son, that guided him to crawl, to walk,
and draw his letters down a slate,

"Rough hands that held the plow
to virgin soil, held the Bible book,
the ragged hymnal page, and held
a cooling cloth against her throat
and trembled the dark tonic
to her spoon,
then clasped in prayer
that she might live.

"These the hands that took her hands
in joy as springtimes came and went
as summer waned
and snowy winds roared in.
These the hands locked tightly
at his knees, rheumy hands
that ached with time's old ache.

"And these, the blue-veined callused
hands clasped at his chest at last
as he lies in his narrow bed
where prairie winds blow in
and the sweet smell of blue
and yellow blossoms drifts on

58

the soft air that blows
over his narrow bed.

"These the hands
that God will clasp.
Amen."

§§§§§§§§§

And Jason remains for the funeral feast,
stays the night, sleeping
on a pallet on the gallery.

At morning, someone lends him
a horse, and he travels back
to his home.

"Where have you been?" his people
ask. "You have been ill. Are you
well now? We closed the house,
cared for your horse. We will
bring her back. We will bring
food. We need you."

He goes to Alice's grave.
Grass is weaving its green mat
again. Only a bit of red earth
awaits its cover.

How long ago did he stand here
in desolation? There is no way
to count the days.
The resurrection fern springs
near the rose bush where
one red rose is blooming.

59

He has wandered in his wilderness
and returned. He sees life
in the red rose.

§§§§§§§§§

Now, Jason comes to Caleb's house again
to gather all the nearby friends
for preaching and for prayer,
but when he rides up
in the yard
and ties his horse,
Ruth comes to the door,
Ebenezer's daughter,
and Jason is surprised.

"Last time I saw you," he begins,
but Ruth takes up the sentence
and she says, "You read a letter
Caleb sent me. I had you write
my answer to him."

"And so?" Jason asks.
Caleb's old hound dog
comes wagging his long tail
and whines a welcome
for the visitor.

"We pledged our troth
before our friends and God,
for, pastor, you were nowhere
to be found."

He nods sadly. "I was nowhere
to be found. But gentle Ruth,
I've found myself. And now,
this evening when the word gets 'round

that I am here for preaching and for
prayer, we'll have a wedding
for you."

Jason looks off to the field
where Caleb sees him, waves
and turns around his plow
to head for home.
And Jason walks out to greet
the bridegroom with a smile.

§§§§§§§§§

"Resin on the bow
And around we go.
Swing your girl
And do-se-do.

"Fiddle is fast
Fiddle is sweet
And stomp! go
The dancing feet!"

Outside in the dark
On his lonely way,
Jason now sees
His people at play

And the music beats
Out his loneliness.
A brown haired girl
In calico dress

Dances each dance
Fast as can be.
He thinks the girl
Could be Emily

Who trusted no man
In those days ago,
But wearily he
Now turns to go

With the song's quick call
In his beating blood,
But he must discount
His mounting mood.

He rides into
The forest night
With his heart soon sad
And his heart soon light.

§§§§§§§§§

LOG-ROLLING, QUILTING-BEE

Deep in the jasmine air, the jasmine
air, the brown butterfly flies
and the wasp flies too,
while the green lizard frisks about
and the old frog sleeps by the stream.

All the uncles and nephews are here
trimming down logs and raising
four walls for the house
of a betrothed couple.
How they laugh and tell whispered
jokes until Jason rides up.
But he rolls up his sleeves
and goes to work mixing adobe
to close all the chinks.

62

There in the distant house
all the women have come,
and they sit in slat-back chairs
around a quilting frame
they have swung on ropes
from the ceiling. In and out
got the needles, to weave
into narrow ridges
the blocks of a "Log Cabin" quilt
the women are making today
to give to the bride.

Out back, venison is roasting
and there will be corn cakes and squash
and sour-sweet pies of rhubarb.

Children are noisy at play
in the clearing, their bare feet
swift on the grass. And the lazy cats
drowse with one eye open.

Tables are set under the oaks
and when the sun stands at meridian
and when the men have washed
in the bayou, they come hungrily
to the feast. The twit of a redbird
is heard, and the low cooing
of Apache doves,
and when Jason walks up,
rolling his sleeves down,
he sees Emily, who has come
from afar for the celebration,
Emily who held a gun on him once.

In the instant before others gather,
no word is spoken between them
but their eyes meet and hold.

They stand, staring in the moment
of their future, they stand staring
in the moment of their joy.

§§§§§§§§§

UNDER THE ARBOR

Through the green
and the untrammeled woodlands,
through the mornings and evenings
they come, and some are coming
on horses, and some are riding
in wagons, and others
are walking along.

Their voices ring through the forest
as they sing their joy at their journey,
for soon they will camp by the river
and soon they will cook by the river
and soon they will sleep
under the stars. They will sleep
to the murmuring song of the river
and the song of the mockingbird.

Over there in the clearing,
the old men and young men are building
of saplings and palmetto branches
an open church in the wildwood.

Here in the aura of morning
and here in the evening's torchlight
the women and children and men
will sit in the shade of the arbor
and hear the stories of heaven.

And here they will rise in their fervor
and their voices will ring to the heavens
and here they will come to be washed

of their sins, here in the green
and the untrammeled forest,
here at the river of life.

§§§§§§§§§

Jason is leading the singing
when out of the clear blue evening,
out of the starry evening,
out of the perfume of honeysuckle
and the lemony smell of magnolia,
out of the chorus of voices
singing out words as he leads them,
suddenly, sweeter than honey
made by the little black bees,
and clearer even
that the gentle song of the river

comes a voice as fresh as the morning,
a voice ringing high as the rooftop
and singing along with Jason
so all other voices are stopping,
and all other eyes are turning
to the slender young singer
among them
with her brown hair tied up
in a ribbon, and herself demure
in calico.

Jason's voice stops on a note
and he pauses there in the singing,
for the singer, he sees, is Emily,
and she has come to be with him.
She has come into the fold.

§§§§§§§§§

66

Night fell, and there beside
   the river's bend,
He built his supper fire
   and made his camp.
He watched the lingering light
   on water end
And saw the slim moon hang
   her fragile lamp.

He laid aside his old black
   coat and hat
And knelt down in the pine straw,
   bowed his head
To say a prayer, and for awhile,
   he sat
Before he spread a blanket
   for his bed.

He saw the stars that sugared up
   the sky
And in the dark, the music
   that he heard
Came from the river noises
   and the high
Sweet repertory of a
   mockingbird.

He closed his eyes and thought
   of families
Hard bitten by rough work
   and early end,
By summer's furnace heat
   and winter's freeze
And all the trials a frontier life
   could send.

He married, baptized,
    and he buried them,
He held their hands, imploring
    God to bless.
He read the Scriptures, pointing out
    each gem,
And heard the folks who thought
    they must confess.

For weeks along the circuit,
    riding through
The rivers and the swamplands
    and the mud,
He fought the flies
    and the mosquitoes too,
But oh, he saw each flower
    deep in bud!

Bone-weary, soon he'd close
    the circle fast
For he'd be riding homeward
    to his place.
His wife and children he would see
    at last...
He longed to kiss each one's
    beloved face.

Worn Bible in his hands, his lips
    in prayer,
He rested in the promise
    of God's care.

§§§§§§§§§

Violette Newton is a Poet Laureate of Texas, recipient of the Medwick Award from the Poetry Society of America, as well as other poetry honors, including book publication awards. She has won recognition for book reviewing and for short fiction writing and is a member of the Southeast Texas Women's Hall of Fame. In 1994, the Poetry Society of Texas gave her its highest honor, voted on by members, the Hilton Ross Greer Award, for years of service to the society and to poetry. JASON'S JOURNEY is her fifteenth book.